Occasional Paper 115

Westminster Kings

and the medieval Palace of Westminster

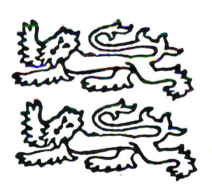

John Cherry and Neil Stratford
edited by Neil Stratford

Department of Medieval and Later Antiquities 1995

BRITISH MUSEUM OCCASIONAL PAPERS

Publishers: The British Museum
                Great Russell Street
                London WC1B 3DG

Production Editor: Josephine Turquet

Distributors: British Museum Press
                46 Bloomsbury Street
                London WC1B 3QQ

Occasional Paper No. 115, 1995
Westminster Kings and the medieval Palace of Westminster
by John Cherry and Neil Stratford, edited by Neil Stratford

ISBN 0 86159 115 1
ISSN 0142 4815

For a complete catalogue giving information on the full range of available Occasional Papers, please write to:
The Marketing Assistant
British Museum Press
46 Bloomsbury Street
London WC1B 3QQ

Printed and bound by Chameleon Press Ltd.

TO HOWARD COLVIN

CONTENTS

Preface   vii

Acknowledgements   viii

Bibliography   ix

Westminster Kings   1

The medieval Palace of Westminster   2

The Antiquaries and Architects   8

The Painted Chamber of Henry III   11

    The decoration of the Painted Chamber of Henry III   17

Edward III and St. Stephen's Chapel   28

    Fragments of wall-paintings   34

    St. Stephen's Chapel - the altar-wall   44

King William II's Hall   50

    The Romanesque capitals from William Rufus' Hall   56

Richard II's rebuilding of the Norman Hall   61

    Richard II and the Westminster Kings   68

    Conservation of the kings   73

    The north façade of Westminster Hall   74

Heraldry and badges   92

    Badges   92

    Seals   95

    Quadrants   96

    Ewers   98

Westminster Hall after the Middle Ages   101

The Fire of 1834   107

Preface

The exhibition *Westminster Kings and the Medieval Palace of Westminster*, at the British Museum from 1st November 1995 to 14th January 1996, was mounted in a very short space of time. It was not possible to produce a catalogue to coincide with the opening. However, many visitors and not least a number of the institutions which lent to the exhibition expressed a wish for a permanent record of the event. This *Occasional Paper* is published to meet this wish.

The reader's indulgence is therefore craved. The volume's contents were chosen to make an exhibition, not a book. The captions beneath the plates were written as exhibition labels. The longer passages of text are taken from the information panels designed and laid out to allow the visitor to the exhibition to 'follow the story'. One particular cause for regret: dimensions of the paintings, sculpture, watercolours and drawings were not able to be included because the proposal to publish the exhibition came too late for accurate measurements to be taken. I myself wrote the majority of the text and labels, John Cherry the section devoted to heraldry and badges, while Martin Royalton-Kisch drafted the label for the early 17th-century view of Westminster Hall (p. 102).

A list of lending institutions and of those who helped the authors can be found at the end of the volume. A particular debt of gratitude is owed to Dr Christopher Wilson, who kindly read the exhibition copy and pointed out several errors, although he is by no means responsible for those which no doubt still remain. The authors have dedicated this book to Sir Howard Colvin; without his remarkable archival researches, published in the first volume of *The King's Works* (1963) and in *Architectural History* (1966), the exhibition would have been impossible to put on.

The great lost buildings of the past exert a strong fascination. Westminster Palace is one of them. Already in the late 18th and early 19th century, scholars and antiquaries were studying and drawing the surviving parts of the Palace. They are the heroes of this volume. One day I hope that a more comprehensive exhibition with a full catalogue will be mounted, to cover the lesser-known parts of the medieval and Tudor palace of Westminster, not just the three buildings (The Painted chamber, St. Stephen's Chapel and the Great Hall) which are the subject of this volume.

Neil Stratford
Keeper of Medieval and Later Antiquities

Acknowledgements

The Trustees of the British Museum in collaboration with the House of Lords and the House of Commons wish to thank the following, who generously lent to the exhibition:

Her Majesty The Queen
Mr J. Auld
The British Library (Department of Manuscripts and Map Library)
The Dorset County Museum
English Heritage
Guildhall Library, Corporation of London
The Leeds City Museum and the Prince of Wales's Own Regiment of Yorkshire
The Museum of London (Medieval Collections and Paintings, Prints and Drawings Collections)
Sir John Soane's Museum
The Society of Antiquaries of London
The Tate Gallery
The Victoria and Albert Museum (Prints, Drawings and Paintings Collections)
The Dean, Sub- Dean, and Chapter of Westminster Abbey
Westminster City Archives
The Yorkshire Museum

Others generously advised with the contents of the exhibition:

Paul Binski
Lorne Cambell
Mary Clapinson
Alice Davis
George Henderson
Françoise Jestaz
The Hamilton Kerr Institute
The Director and Staff of the National Gallery
Martin Royalton-Kisch
Gregory Rubinstein
Keith Taylor of Taylor Pearce Restoration Services Ltd
Clive and Jane Wainwright
The Staff of the Library and Muniments of Westminster Abbey
Christopher Wilson
George Zarnecki

Permission to reproduce the photographs is gratefully acknowledged to the lenders, and the Bodleian Library, Oxford.

Summary Bibliography

Note: Entries within the sections are given in chronological order of publication.
Those works that are cited in several sections are referred to in an abbreviated form, given at the end of the bibliographical entry within [   ] brackets.

J. Carter, *The Ancient Architecture of England*, 2 vols. London 1795-1814.

J.T. Smith, *Antiquities of Westminster*, 1st edn. London 1807 (with text in part by J. S. Hawkins); *Additional Plates*, 1809.   [J.T. Smith, 1807]

'Notes and Remarks, by the late Mr William Capon, to accompany his Plan of the ancient Palace of Westminster', read 23rd December 1824, *Vetusta Monumenta*, V, 1835, 1-7, pl. XLVII.   [Capon, 1824]

E.W. Brayley, J. Britton, *The History of the Ancient Palace and late Houses of Parliament at Westminster*, London 1836.

I.M. Cooper, 'The meeting places of Parliament in the ancient Palace of Westminster', *Journal of the British Archaeological Association*, 3rd ser., III, 1938, 97-138.   [Cooper, 1938]

ed. H.M. Colvin, *The History of the King's Works*, London HMSO, vol. 1: *The Middle Ages*, 3 vols (1963); vol. VI: *1782-1851* (1973).   [Colvin, 1963,1973]

ed. H.M. Colvin, 'Views of the old Palace of Westminster', *Architectural History*, 9, 1966, 21-184.   [Colvin, 1966]

R.J.B. Walker, 'The Palace of Westminster after the fire of 1834', *Walpole Society*, 44, 1972-74, 94-122.

P.M. Rogers, 'Medieval fragments from the old Palace of Westminster in the Sir John Soane Museum', *Parliamentary History, Libraries and Records. Essays presented to Maurice Bond*, House of Lords Record Office, 1981.

Age of Chivalry. Art in Plantagenet England 1200-1400, ed. J. Alexander, P. Binski, Royal Academy of Arts, London 1987.   [*Age of Chivalry*, 1987]

The Painted Chamber

J.T. Smith, 1807, *passim*.

'Discoveries in the Painted Chamber', *Gentleman's Magazine*, 1819 (2), 389-92.

Capon, 1824.

J.G. Rokewode, 'A memoir on the Painted Chamber in the Palace at Westminster', read 12th May 1842, *Vetusta Monumenta*, VI, 1885, 1-37, pls. XXVI-XXXIX, (designs by C.A. Stothard).

Colvin, 1963, 494-502.

Colvin, 1966, 43- 6, 146-65.

P. Binski, *The Painted Chamber at Westminster*, Society of Antiquaries, London 1986.

M. Liversidge, P. Binski, J. Lynn, 'Two ceiling fragments from the Painted Chamber at Westminster Palace', *Burlington Magazine*, August 1995, 491-501.

St Stephen's Chapel

J. Topham, *Some Account of the Collegiate Chapel of St. Stephen, Westminster*, with *Plans, Elevations, Sections and Specimens of the Architecture and Ornaments of the remaining parts... engraved... from drawings... by J. Carter*, Society of Antiquaries, 1795; issued with 14 additional plates by J. Dixon, R. Smirke and Sir G. Naylor, commentary by Sir H.C. Englefield, Society of Antiquaries 1811.

J.T. Smith, 1807, *passim*.

F. Mackenzie, *The Architectural Antiquities of the Collegiate Chapel of St Stephen*, London 1844.

C.L. Kingsford, 'Our Lady of the Pew. The King's Oratory or Closet in the Palace of Westminster', read 7th December 1916, *Archaeologia*, LXVIII, 1916-17, 1-20.

M. Hastings, *St Stephen's Chapel and its place in the development of the Perpendicular style in England*, Cambridge 19 55.

Colvin, 1963, 510-25.

Colvin, 1966, 42-3, 137-45.

M. Galinou, 'Adam Lee's drawings of St Stephen's Chapel, Westminster. Antiquarianism and showmanship in early 19th-century London', *Transactions of the London and Middlesex Archaeological Society*, XXXIV, 1983, 231-44.

Age of Chivalry, 1987, 79-82,337-9 (nos. 324-5) (by C. Wilson), 498-9 (no. 680) (by D. Park), 499-500 (no. 681) (by P. Binski).

The Great Hall

'Remarks on the architectural History of Westminster Hall: in a letter from Sydney Smirke, Esq. F.S.A., to Sir Henry Ellis, K.H., F.R.S. Secretary', read 28th May 1835, *Archaeologia*, XXVI, 1836, 406-14, 'Second Letter... ', read 4th February 1836, *ibid.*, 415-21.

'A further Account of the original Architecture of Westminster Hall. In a letter from Sydney Smirke, Esq. F.S.A. to Sir Henry Ellis, K.H., F.R.S. Secretary', read 2nd February 1837, *Archaeologia*, XXVII, 1838, 135-9.

I.M. Cooper, 'Westminster Hall', *Journal of the British Archaeological Association*, 3rd ser., I, 1937, 168-228.

Colvin, 1963, 42-8, 527-33.

Colvin, 1966, 33-6, 76-93,99.

Colvin, 1973, 497-503 (by M.H. Port).

English Romanesque Art 1066-1200, Arts Council of Great Britain, 1984, 154-5 (no. 105) (by G. Zarnecki).

L.T. Courtenay, 'The Westminster Hall roof and its 14th-century sources', *Journal of the Society of Architectural Historians*, XLIII, 1984, 295-309.

C. Wilson, *Age of Chivalry*, 1987, 506-8 (no. 692).

M. Hay, *Westminster Hall and the Medieval Kings*, London 1995.

The fire of 1834

K. Solander, *Dreadful fire! Burning of the Houses of Parliament*, Catalogue of the exhibition, Cleveland Museum of Art, 1984.

Badges, seals, quadrants, jewellery, ewers

J. Cherry, 'The Dunstable Swan Jewel', *Journal of the British Archaeological Association*, XXXII, 1969, 38-53.

G. L'E. Turner, 'Charles Whitwell's addition, c. 1595, to a fourteenth century quadrant', *Antiquaries Journal*, LXV, 1985, 454-5.

Age of Chivalry, 1987.

B. Spencer, *Pilgrim souvenirs and secular badges*, Salisbury and South Wiltshire Museum Medieval Catalogue part 2, Salisbury 1990.

M. Bailey, 'Two Kings, their arms and some jugs', *Apollo*, Dec. 1993, 387-90.

D. Gordon, *The Wilton Diptych*, London 1993.

J. Cherry, *The Middleham Jewel and Ring*, York 1995.

WESTMINSTER KINGS

Westminster today   Photo Woodmansterne

The Medieval Palace of Westminster

Westminster was only one of many royal palaces, but it was among the chief residences of the monarch from the time of Edward the Confessor to Henry VIII. This publication concentrates on three of the palace buildings about which most is known. The Painted Chamber was the king's bedroom and audience chamber, combining privacy with important semi-public meetings. St. Stephen's Chapel was the main place of worship, served by a college of canons. The Great Hall was where ceremonial events such as coronation feasts could be mounted, but for most of this time it also housed the Royal Courts of Justice. The Hall also served as a vestibule to adjoining rooms used by the Exchequer and the King's Council Chamber (Star Chamber).

Parliaments were sporadic and held wherever the king might be. From the 14th century onwards their sessions took place in the Painted Chamber. Under Henry VIII Whitehall Palace took over as the royal residence, and Westminster became the principal seat of Parliament and the Law Courts. From 1548, St. Stephen's Chapel ceased to be a place of worship and became the House of Commons. The Lords were housed in another medieval room to the south.

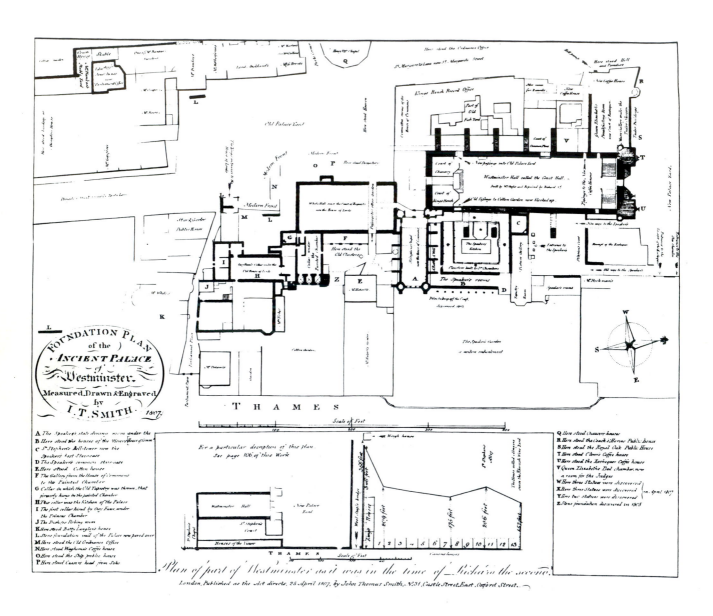

Plan of the Palace of Westminster from J.T. Smith, *Antiquities of Westminster*, 1807

English medieval palaces grew piecemeal as time passed, and as needs and tastes changed. They were not permanent places of residence for the Court, which moved with the seasons from one royal house to another. Westminster was like the other palaces in this respect, but its position on the river near London, one of the biggest commercial centres of medieval Europe, gave it unique status.

During the 12th century, Westminster became the seat of the royal treasury and the Norman kings all built here. William Rufus' Hall, nearly 73 metres in length, remains to this day one of the largest secular buildings of the Middle Ages. Offices, chambers, chapels and accommodation were all fitted into the marshy area of land between the river and the precinct of Westminster Abbey. Surrounded by walls and tower-gateways, the palace stood to the west of London complementing the royal stronghold of the Tower of London, to the east. Services and storage were on the ground floor, high-status official or ceremonial rooms on the first floor.

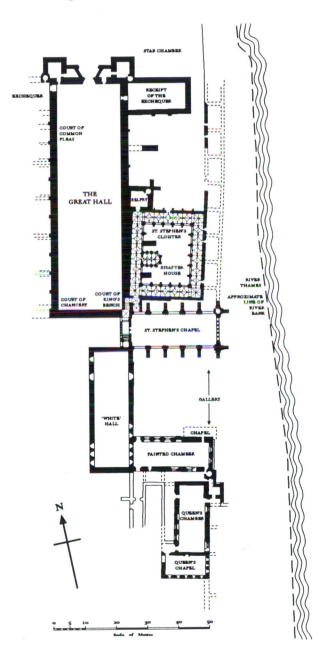

Schematic plan of the main Palace buildings at the end of the Middle Ages

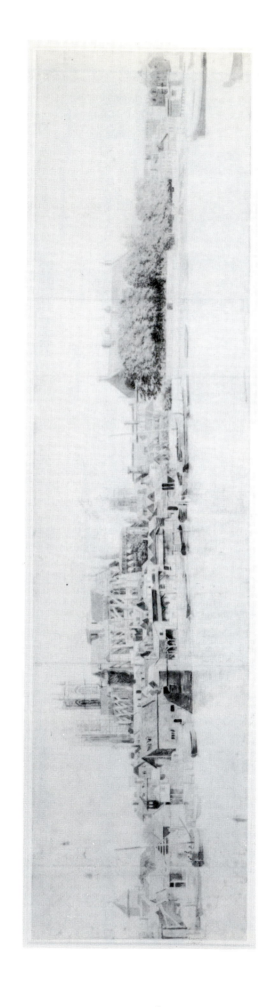

Panorama of Westminster from the river Watercolour, by Samuel Scott, 1739   British Museum, P&D 1865-8-10-1323
Samuel Scott (1702?-1772) produced a number of celebrated views of the Thames. This view of Westminster is taken from the south-east, with the embankment and riverside life in the foreground (on the left), the Abbey beyond and the Hall (on the right) hidden behind trees.

Westminster Palace from the river Watercolour, by Peter de Wint, about 1810 Victoria and Albert Museum, P61-1921
de Wint (1784-1849) shows the river front and the Palace from the north-east, with the Abbey in the distance. The Hall dominates the Palace (on the right). The east façade and gable of St. Stephen's Chapel, regothicised by James Wyatt around 1800, are prominent (in the centre).

The Antiquaries and Architects

From the 17th century onwards there was great interest in the buildings of the medieval palace. The period of passionate interest among antiquaries began about 1780 and only ended in the sad aftermath of the fire. It is thanks to the accurate studies of these artists and scholars that we know so much about the old palace; those whose work is illustrated here include John Carter, William Capon, J.T. Smith, Richard and Sidney Smirke, Sir John Soane, Edward Crocker, Adam Lee and Charles Stothard. There were many others, as well as a group of official artists who recorded the surviving buildings after the fire of 1834.

The present Houses of Parliament, principally the work of Charles Barry and Augustus Welby Pugin, were erected for the most part between 1839 and 1860. Barry's design using the late Gothic or 'Perpendicular' style was chosen by a select committee as being in harmony with the old buildings, although in the event most of these were demolished to accommodate the new plan.

View of the ruins of St. Stephen's looking east, after 1834　　　Palace of Westminster

8

Panorama of the ruins of the old Palace of Westminster after the fire Oil on paper supported by canvas, by George Scharf, after 1834 Palace of Westminster, 3793, purchased in 1993 by the Advisory Committee on Works of Art in the House of Commons

George Scharf (1788-1860) came to London from his native Bavaria in 1816. Most of his early works in England were topographical and he is known to have worked occasionally in the Palace from 1818 onwards. Following the fire, he was drawn to record the medieval ruins, which particularly suited his artistic temperament. St. Stephen's Chapel is a roofless cage of walls (on the right) but the cloister of St. Stephen's is substantially intact (in the centre). The medieval cloister was rebuilt in the reign of Henry VIII, but survived in spirit as the Cloister Court in Barry's Houses of Parliament, after 1839.

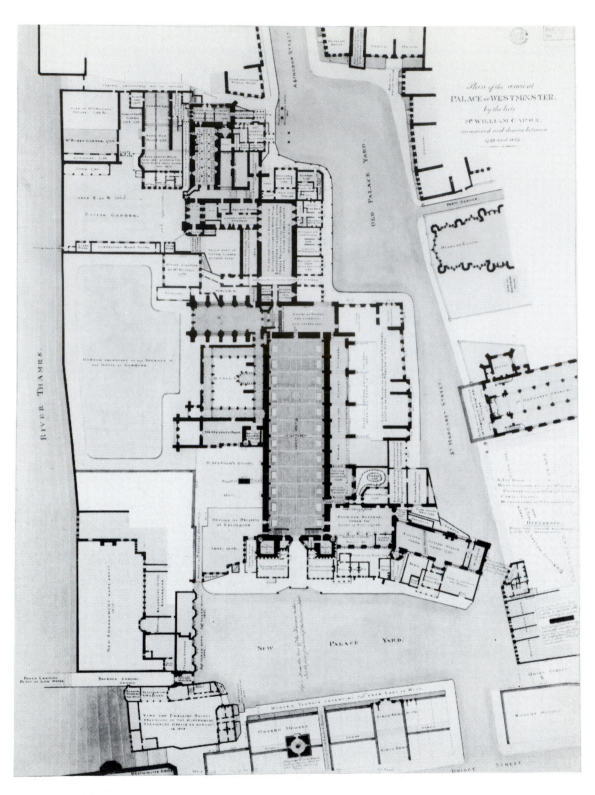

Plan of the ancient Palace of Westminster   Pen and ink, pencil and watercolour, by William Capon, based on measurements and drawings executed between 1793-1823   Westminster City Archives, Box 56, no. 9
This important document was engraved for the Society of Antiquaries in *Vetusta Monumenta V* (1835). It records the dates of various changes to the palace in the period preceding the fire of 1834. The plan is orientated with north towards the bottom. The Hall is marked <u>A</u>, the crypt of St. Stephen's Chapel <u>D</u> and the undercroft of the Painted Chamber is labelled parallel to the Chapel, further south. William Capon (1757-1827) was among the most active of the antiquaries who studied the Palace from the 1780s onwards.

The Painted Chamber of Henry III

During his long reign (1216-72) Henry III often resided at Westminster, where he spent lavishly on the new abbey church as well as the palace. To the south of St. Stephen's Chapel his great chamber, an older Norman structure on two floors, was extensively rebuilt and decorated with wall-paintings. By the early 14th century the first-floor room was already known as the Painted Chamber.

The Painted Chamber was the king's state bedchamber, with a private chapel alongside it, and could be used for audiences and even Parliaments from the 14th century onwards. It was 24.5 metres long by 7.9 metres wide and 9.7 metres high. Henry III, early in his reign, gave it elegant Gothic tracery windows which commanded a view of the Thames.

Henry III – detail of his bronze effigy in Westminster Abbey, 1291

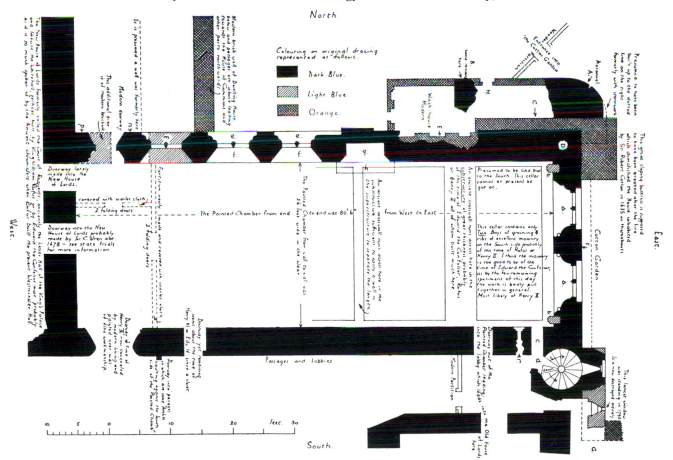

Plan of the Painted Chamber by William Capon 1795, 1799, 1818 (as published by Cooper, 1938)

View of the interior of the Painted Chamber, looking east   Watercolour, by William Capon, 1799   Society of Antiquaries of London

This, and the following view, justly famous, were executed eleven years after John Carter first recorded the interior of the Chamber. In 1799 the room acted as the vestibule to the House of Lords. Capon's precision of detail is valuable, particularly for the ceiling with the wooden *paterae*, the tracery windows and the tapestries of the Trojan War, now lost, which were probably made about 1470. Vestiges of the medieval wall-paintings can be seen beneath the plastered rendering on the upper walls, although their full extent was not to be revealed until some twenty years later.

View of the interior of the Painted Chamber, looking west   Watercolour, by William Capon, 1799   Society of
Antiquaries of London
See the previous view for Capon's watercolour, looking east in 1799.

The exterior of the Painted Chamber, from the north-east   Watercolour, signed *Nash*, about 1800-1810   Guildhall Library, Corporation of London

The watercolourist Frederick Nash (1782-1856) was active in Westminster Abbey and Palace from 1800 onwards. In 1807 he was appointed architectural draughtsman to the Society of Antiquaries. This view is precious as a record of the state of the Chamber and adjoining buildings in the very first years of the 19th century. The two east windows of the Chamber appear to have been given 'Perpendicular' tracery about 1800, although they were restored to their original 13th-century appearance after 1816. The 13th-century remains of the north wall are shown, including the oval-shaped windows of the king's oratory.

The decoration of the Painted Chamber of Henry III

Following a fire in 1263, Henry III ordered the redecoration of the Painted Chamber. The scheme included a wooden ceiling studded with flat geometric panels (*paterae*). Alongside the windows were painted huge figures of the Virtues and Vices. Above the head of the king's bed was a large painting of 1266-7 showing the Coronation of his canonised predecessor, Edward the Confessor, to whom he was particularly devoted. Under Edward I, probably in the 1290s, a cycle of Old Testament scenes, including numerous battle episodes, was painted around the walls.

The room and its decorations were studied and recorded in the 1780s and 1790s by John Carter and William Capon, and later by other antiquaries, particularly Charles Stothard for the Society of Antiquaries. Much is therefore known about the paintings. They were thought to be totally destroyed in the 1834 fire.

However in 1993 two panels from the ceiling were discovered in Bristol. A note on the back records their history: in 1816 they were removed from the ceiling of the Painted Chamber by Adam Lee, 'Labourer in Trust', working with the Clerk of Works to the Palace of Westminster, when the room was being restored. Lee worked for many years in the Houses of Parliament and his large painting of St. Stephen's Chapel is also illustrated.

Confirmation that the panels come from the ceiling is given by the surviving wood *patera* (illustrated here); judging by the position of the pin-holes, such *paterae* must have covered over a set of painted panels of which these are two. Apparently Henry III's redecoration of the room after the 1263 fire envisaged a scheme of figurative paintings on the ceiling, which was soon abandoned in favour of the decorative *paterae*, themselves probably richly coloured.

Adam Lee is known to have possessed four ceiling panels from the Painted Chamber: a seraph, and three prophets, Isaiah, Jeremiah and Jonah. The Seraph and (perhaps) Jeremiah are those found in Bristol. Painted on oak in an oil medium, they seem to be the earliest surviving English panel paintings. They are probably part of the scheme executed in the 1260s by the King's Painter, Master Walter of Durham. Their exceptional condition and the beauty of their line-drawing can best be judged by x-rays, and they are closely comparable in style to contemporary English manuscript illumination.

Seraph from the ceiling of Henry III's Painted Chamber   Oil medium on oak planks with areas of stamped decoration, after 1263   British Museum, MLA 1995, 4-1,1. Purchased with the aid of grants from the National Heritage Memorial Fund and the National Art Collections Fund

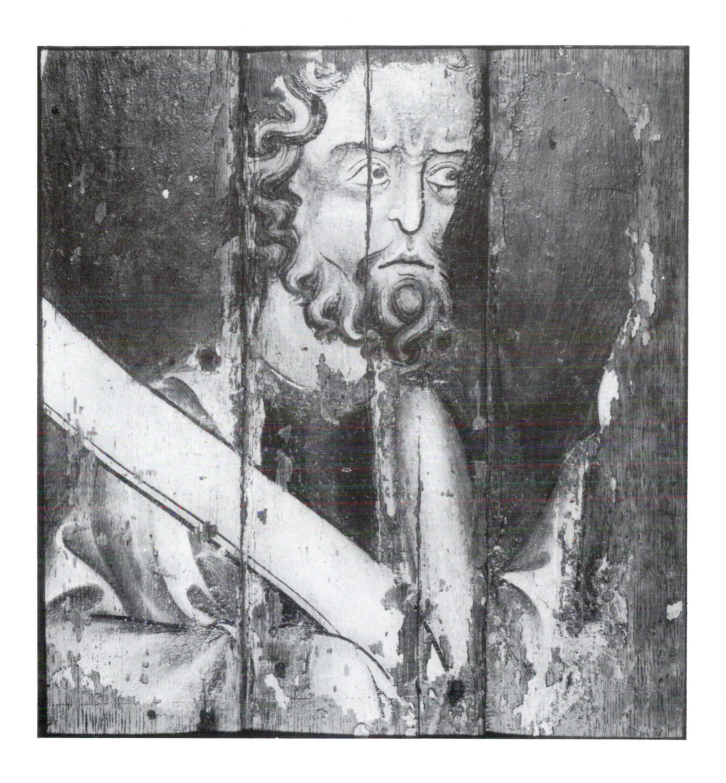

Prophet, perhaps Jeremiah, from the ceiling of Henry III's Painted Chamber Oil medium on oak planks, after 1263
British Museum, MLA 1995, 4-1,2. Purchased with the aid of grants from the National Heritage Memorial Fund and
the National Art Collections Fund

Panel from the Painted Chamber, X-ray of the Prophet   C. Hurst, Hamilton Kerr Institute

Oxford, Bodleian Library, Douce MS. 180, page 33: the angel gives St. John the book to eat (Apocalypse, X, 8-9)
The panels provide unique evidence of the quality of the work in the Painted Chamber, and with the comparable manuscripts confirm that the mid-thirteenth century was one of the high points of English medieval art. The Seraph is stylistically close to this manuscript of about 1270.

Moscow, State Library MS. ИН 1678, leaf from an Apocalypse, about 1260-65: St. John preaching
Compare the Prophet on the Painted Chamber ceiling panel.

Panel from the ceiling of the Painted Chamber
Oak, formerly painted, with pinholes for attachment to the ceiling, after 1263. Sir John Soane's Museum, M 363

The 1837 records of Sir John Soane's Museum call this, 'A shield from the Ceiling of the Painted Chamber at Westminster taken down at the time of the General Repair of that Room in 1819.' Described as *paterae* (lit. dish) in the early 19th-century accounts of the Chamber's ceiling, a set of such oak panels was put up at an early date to cover over oil paintings (including the Seraph and the Prophet). The paintings seem to have formed part of a scheme, apparently begun after a fire in 1263, and soon abandoned in favour of the *paterae*. Edward Crocker (about 1757-1836) as Clerk of the Works was in charge of restoring the room in 1819, to become the Court of Claims.

Painted and gilded wooden rosette, said to come from the Painted Chamber 15th-16th century Sir John Soane's Museum, M 118

The original function of this rosette is not known, although the 1837 records of Sir John Soane's Museum state that it comes from the Painted Chamber.

The Coronation of Edward the Confessor (*Cest Le Coronement Seint Edeward*) Copy of one of the lost wall-paintings in the Painted Chamber Watercolour, by Charles Stothard, 1819 Society of Antiquaries of London

The original was over 3 metres wide. It was situated on the north wall at the east end, behind the king's bed. The quatrefoil opening in the bottom right corner allowed the king to look through into the little oratory behind his bed. The painting was probably executed in 1266-7 by Henry III's painter, Master Walter of Durham, who at this time was paid for 'pictures around the king's bed'.

Charles Stothard (1786-1821) was commissioned by the Society of Antiquaries to record the paintings soon after their full extent became apparent during the restoration works of 1818-19. His watercolours give a lively and apparently accurate rendering of the various lost cycles. Four are illustrated here.

(left) **The Virtue, Largesse (*Largesce*) triumphing over Covetousness (*Covoitise*)**   Society of Antiquaries of London
The original was over 3 metres high and decorated one of the window splays on the south wall.. The arms in the border are England and the Empire. The Virtues and Vices probably belonged to Henry III's decoration of the room after the fire of 1263.

(right) **The Virtue, Meekness (*Debonerete*) triumphing over the Vice, Wrath (*Ira*)** Society of Antiquaries of London
The original was huge like *Largesse* and faced it on the other splay of one of the south windows. The Virtue carries a shield with the arms of England differenced by two bars, while other arms, those of England, the Confessor and St. Edmund are included in the border.

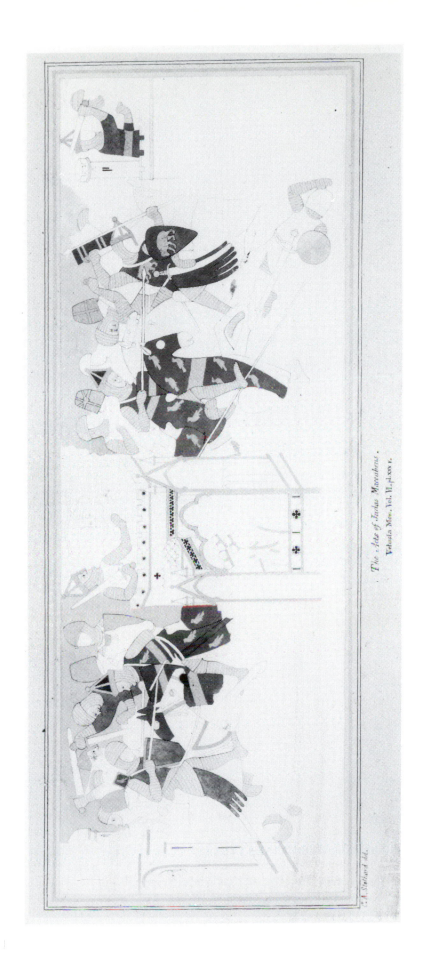

The Acts of Judas Maccabeus.
Vetusta Mon. Vol. VI, pl. xxv v.

T. A. Stothard del.

Two episodes from the Book of Maccabees: Judas Maccabeus in battle against Nicanor (1 Macc., 7). Society of Antiquaries of London
Scenes in two registers from various books of the Old Testament, mostly of battles and other military subject-matter, were painted on the north and south walls.
It has been suggested that this cycle was executed for Edward I in the 1290s.

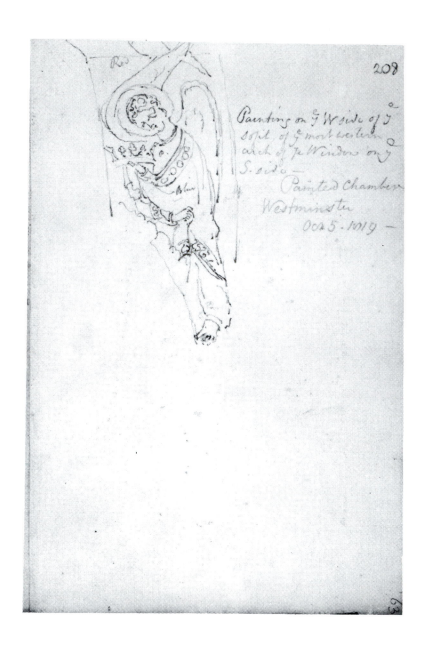

Annotated sketch of a lost wall-painting in the Painted Chamber   Pencil and watercolour, by John Buckler, 1819
British Library, Add. MS 36370, fol. 208   By permission of the British Library Board
An angel holding a crown. Buckler notes that the original was painted on the soffit of the westernmost window of the
south wall. The angel was above the Virtue, *Debonerete*. The drawing also has colour notes and is dated 'Oct 5. 1819',
during Edward Crocker's restoration of the Chamber.

Annotated sketches of lost wall-paintings in the Painted Chamber   Pencil and watercolour, by John Buckler, 1819
British Library, Add. MS 36370, fols. 207 (top), 209 (bottom)   By permission of the British Library Board
(top) Architectural notes, inscriptions of the Virtues and Vices and details of two scenes from the history of King
Abimelech (Judges, 9) and, below, from the book of Maccabees (2 Macc., 7). These scenes were part of the Old
Testament cycle and were situated between the two windows on the south wall.
(bottom) Architectural and colour notes, and a sketch of an episode from the history of King Antiochus (2 Macc., 7); part
of this scene is also included in the sketch above, from the south wall of the room.

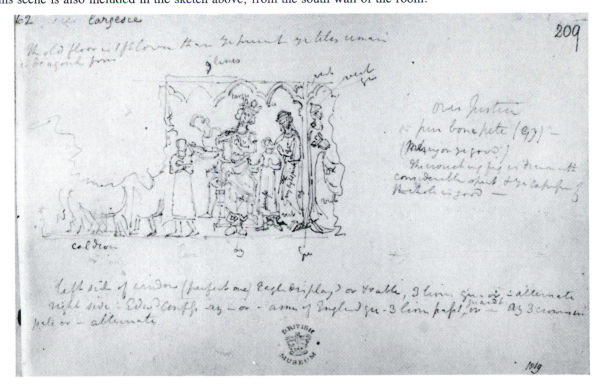

Edward III and St. Stephen's Chapel

St. Stephen's Chapel, the principal palace chapel, was on two levels. The lower chapel was accessible to the royal household and court generally. The more richly decorated main chapel, at first-floor level, was reserved for the royal family and clergy.

The building history of St. Stephen's falls into three periods. The first, for Edward I, from 28 April 1292 to the mid-summer of 1297 was a period of intense activity under the Master Mason, Michael of Canterbury. The crypt which in part survived the 1834 fire was built in the 1290s, though it was drastically remodelled in the 1860s. The second building period lasted from 1320 to the winter of 1325/6 under Edward II.

In the third building period, early in Edward III's reign from 1331 to 1348, most of the upper chapel was constructed. It was decorated between 1349 and 1362. It is however clear that the principal elements of the 1290s' design survived in Edward III's final building. The sculpture, stained-glass and wall-paintings were of extraordinary richness. This must have been one of the most sumptuous interiors of 14th-century Europe.

Coloured statues of angels stood under canopies on the wall-shafts which divided the space into 5 bays lit by large Perpendicular windows. The mouldings and all the surfaces were painted and encrusted with gilded and coloured gesso patterns. Stained glass, grotesque sculptures and painted heraldic shields were accompanied by a huge series of wall-paintings.

Thirty-two standing figures of military saints were painted on the piers, angels four feet high were shown within the wall-arcading and above, in the base of the windows were numerous Biblical scenes. On the altar wall, Edward III, his queen and their children were depicted kneeling beneath the Virgin and Child and scenes of the Infancy of Christ. The painters used huge quantities of linseed oil and the most expensive pigments (including ultramarine and vermilion). By 1548, the chapel had been totally transformed to act as the House of Commons, and its medieval splendour was hidden by Sir Christopher Wren's new interior in the late 17th century.

Edward III   detail of his bronze effigy in Westminster Abbey, late 14th century

A *View of the House of Commons in the Session 1741* Engraving, 'published by J. Pine Sept 29. 1749' Society of Antiquaries of London This celebrated view of the interior of the House of Commons, accompanied by a list of the Speakers from 1259-1747, shows how the medieval architecture of St. Stephen's Chapel was totally masked by Sir Christopher Wren's 17th-century galleries, panelling and rebuilt east window.

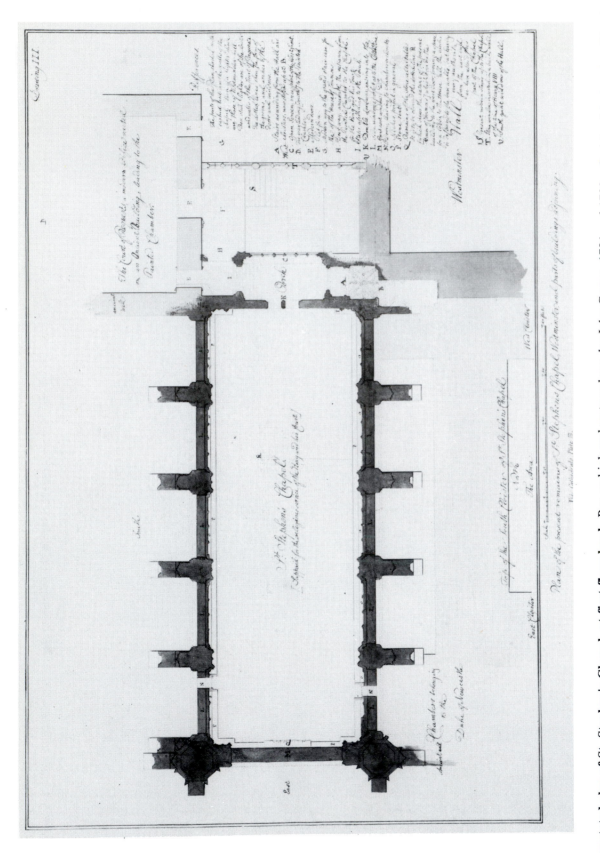

Annotated plan of St. Stephen's Chapel, at first floor level Pen and ink and watercolour, by John Carter, 1791 and 1792 Society of Antiquaries of London John Carter (1748-1817) made a series of carefully laid out and annotated pages of drawings of St. Stephen's Chapel in 1791 and 1792 for the Society of Antiquaries, which they published in 1795, in *Some Account of the Collegiate Chapel of St. Stephen, Westminster* by J. Topham, and others. Although they cannot be relied on in detail, they are invaluable records of the Chapel, prior to James Wyatt's draconian interventions in 1800.

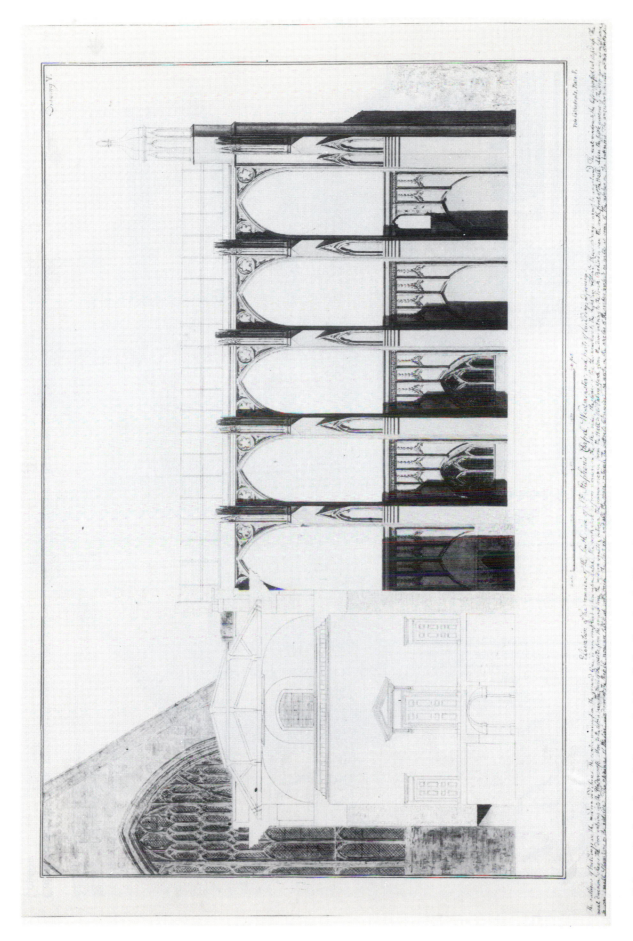

Schematic elevation of the south side of St. Stephen's Chapel, with the south window of Westminster Hall on the left John Carter, 1791 and 1792
Society of Antiquaries of London

Fragments of wall-paintings

St. Stephen's Chapel underwent drastic reconstruction in 1800, when the architect James Wyatt was asked to create extra space in Christopher Wren's House of Commons for new members following the Act of Union with Ireland. A few fragments of the Old Testament scenes, illustrating episodes from the Books of Job and Tobit were rescued at this time; these were presented to the British Museum in 1814 by the Society of Antiquaries.

St. Stephen's Chapel, south-east bay from J.T. Smith, *Antiquities of Westminster*, 1807
J.T. Smith's engraving shows the exact position of the Tobit scenes, in the base of the windows of the most easterly bay on the south side, next to the altar wall and beneath the royal pew. Under the paintings can be seen the pierced and crenellated parapet, of which fragments are also illustrated below. Then came a carved frieze of heraldic shields and supporting beasts. The zone of arcading was painted with angels over a metre high holding textiles.

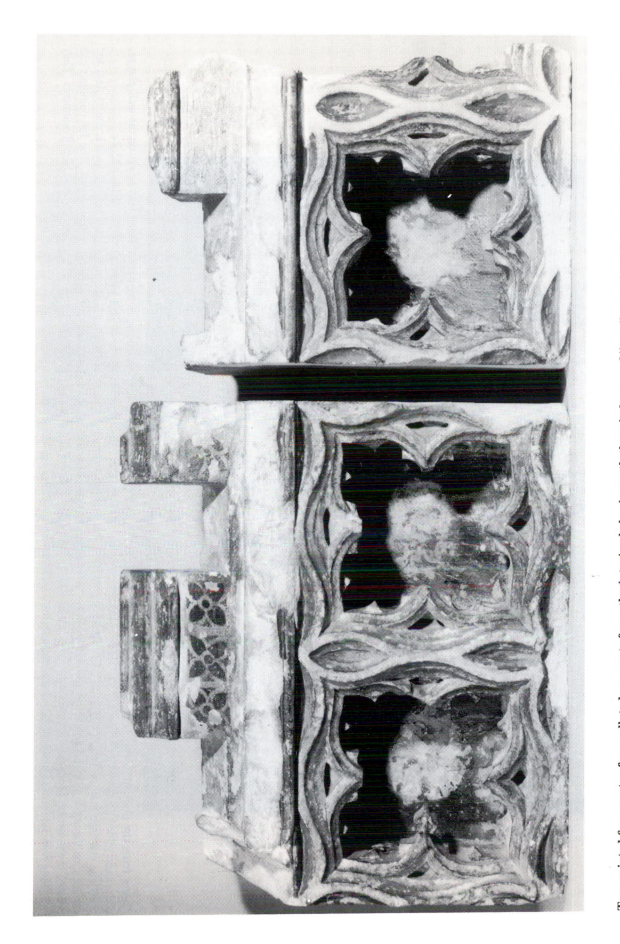

Two painted fragments of crenellated parapet, from the interior ledge beneath the windows   Oil medium, painted between 1350-1363   Presented by the Society of Antiquaries of London British Museum, MLA 1814,3-12,2
Views of the lower walls by J.T. Smith and Robert Smirke show this parapet, which ran above the angels painted within the wall-arcading. A gessoed painted flower filled each opening behind the parapet quatrefoils.

Armorial bearings in St. Stephen's Chapel   Hand-coloured engraved page from J.T. Smith's *Antiquities of Westminster*, dated 1st January 1804, published 1807   Westminster City Archives, Box 57
Painted shields of arms, from above the wall-arcading in the bay near the altar, recorded in 1800

(left) **The east bay of St. Stephen's Chapel, after the fire** Pen and ink and watercolour, by George Moore (?), 1837 Palace of Westminster, 260
This view of the ruined Chapel under scaffolding shows the window in the east bay, north wall and (on the right) the great east window. Painted angels are visible in the 'Perpendicular' panelling of the north-east window, and the fleurs de lys and lions of England on the soffit of the east window.

(right) **The interior of St. Stephen's Chapel, looking west, after the fire** Pen and ink and watercolour, by George Stokes (?), 1836-1837 Palace of Westminster, 1254
The south wall of the Chapel with its heraldic paintings in the soffits of the windows is still standing, the north wall has already been demolished. The Abbey is in the background, the south gable of the Hall on the right.

43

St Stephen's Chapel - the altar-wall

No fragments are known to survive from the altar-wall, but there are unusually precise views of the paintings. J. T. Smith's engraving shows the north section of the wall, beneath the east window, with the Speaker's chair in the centre in the position originally occupied by the high altar. Smith recorded the paintings at the time of the Wyatt demolitions in 1800. The other views shown in this section are part of the record made for the Society of Antiquaries, principally by Richard Smirke.

St Stephen's Chapel - the north side of the altar-wall, with Edward III and the princes (from J.T. Smith, *Antiquities of Westminster*, 1807)

44

St Stephen's Chapel, copy of the paintings on the north half of the altar-wall Tempera and gold leaf on paper, by Richard Smirke, between 1800–1811
Society of Antiquaries of London

Richard Smirke (1778–1815) made a remarkable set of copies of the paintings at the east end of the Chapel for the Society of Antiquaries during Wyatt's demolitions in 1800. He later worked his sketches into highly finished drawings, which were to form the basis for many of the plates in the 1811 volume of the Society on St. Stephen's Chapel. Beneath a fragmentary Adoration of the Magi, the wall to the left of the high altar was decorated with the kneeling Edward III and five of his sons being presented to the Virgin and Child by St. George. The illusionistic effect of these paintings must have been vivid: the figures were set within fictive oratories with windows, behind the real arcading of the chapel.

St Stephen's Chapel, the kneeling Edward III on the altar-wall   Pencil drawing, by Richard Smirke, about 1800
Society of Antiquaries of London
One of Smirke's copies of the altar-wall figures- see the large finished painting by Smirke illustrated on p. 45.

St Stephen's Chapel, Richard Smirke's drawing of the south side of the altar-wall, with Queen Philippa and the princesses, about 1800　　Society of Antiquaries of London

The Queen and her daughters were painted on the wall to the right of the high altar, kneeling beneath scenes of the Infancy of Christ.

(left) **St Stephen's Chapel, the kneeling Queen Philippa on the altar-wall**   Pencil drawing, by Richard Smirke,
about 1800   Society of Antiquaries of London

(right) **St Stephen's Chapel, one of the princesses on the altar-wall**   Watercolour, perhaps by Sir George Naylor,
shortly after 1800   Westminster City Archives, Box 57, no. 88

Smirke's drawing of the Queen and her daughters kneeling to the right of the high altar (reproduced above) allows this
figure to be identified as the third princess kneeling behind the Queen. Another version of this watercolour in the British
Museum records that 'the painting was saved when the havoc was made of many others in various parts of the chapel in
1800.' Therefore the original may still survive.

Perspective view of the interior of St. Stephen's Chapel as it was finished in the reign of King Edward III
Varnished watercolour on paper, by Adam Lee, about 1820-30   Museum of London, A 15454
Adam Lee (about 1772-1843) was employed by the Office of Works in the Palace from 1801 onwards, for some forty years, mostly as Labourer in Trust. His long study of the medieval buildings led to a series of 'Cosmoramic Views and Delineations of the Ancient Palace of Westminster and St. Stephen's Chapel', which was exhibited at the Society of Painters in Water Colours in 1831. In spite of Lee's claim 'to restore views as accurate as possible of those beautiful Edifices', the element of fantastical whimsy is strong: Edward III, Queen Philippa and the Black Prince are admiring the newly completed chapel. Details of the tracery and the general disposition of the architecture rely much on Lee's imagination. Nevertheless this view more than any other evokes the incredible richness of the Chapel's 14th-century decorations.

The Romanesque Capitals from William Rufus' Hall

Presented here are three out of a series of ten capitals, discovered in 1835. They had been reused in the masonry when the Hall was rebuilt in the later 14th century. Their original position is not known. The subject-matter, comprising beasts and scenes of warfare, is appropriate to a secular hall, and can be compared to the near contemporary scenes on the Bayeux Tapestry.

Charles Stothard's copy of the Bayeux Tapestry, published 1819: the attack on the Castle at Dinant

Romanesque capital from William Rufus' Hall: assault on a castle in the form of a tower on stilts, with steps and a gate English Heritage
The figure with an axe and shield on the left is stabbed by the sword of one of the castle's defenders.

57

Romanesque capital from William Rufus' Hall: a lion and an eagle   English Heritage

Romanesque capital from William Rufus' Hall: two scenes with various figures including an ass and a dog   English Heritage

Westminster Hall, as it is today - looking south   Photo: Woodmansterne

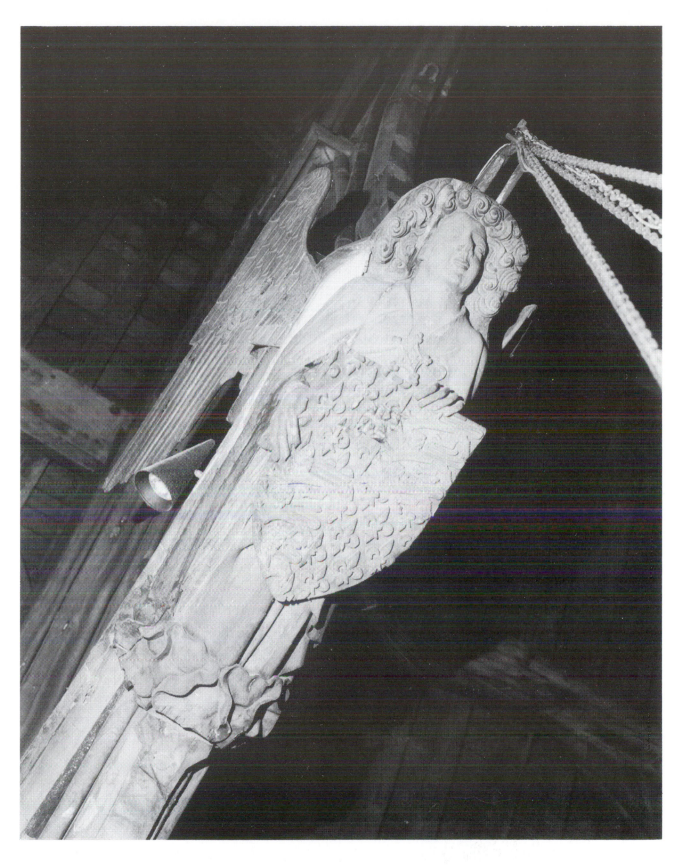

One of the wooden angels projecting from the hammer-beams of the roof. The angel holds the arms of England and was put up in 1396-1397.   Palace of Westminster

Detail of cornice of Richard II's Hall, with the White Hart.

The roof of the Hall   (after Eugène Viollet-le-Duc, *Dictionnaire raisonné de l'architecture française*, 1858-1868)

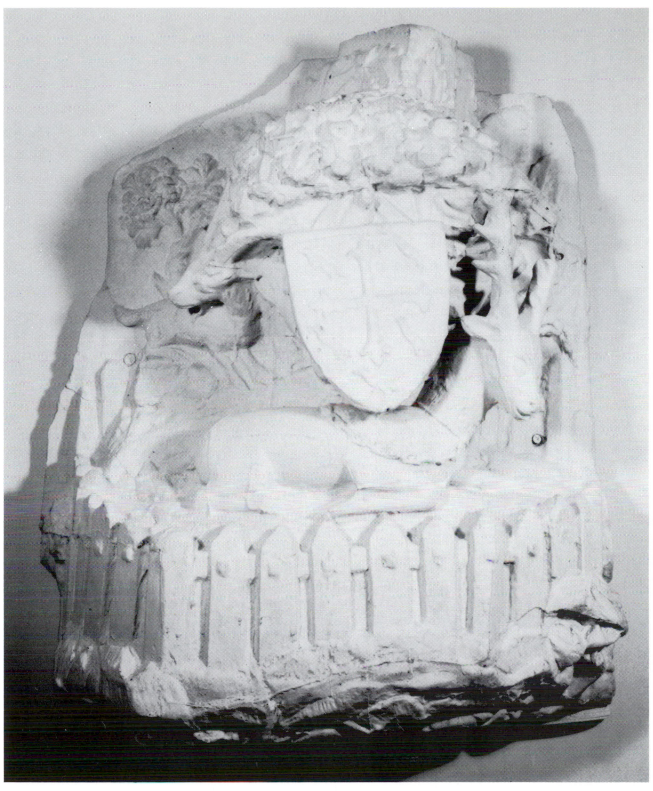

Cast of a corbel which supported the outer arch of the south window of Westminster Hall   Plaster,
made for Sir John Soane, before 1830   Sir John Soane's Museum, M68
The two casts of corbels from the great south window are first recorded in Soane's collection in 1830. Richard II's window was destroyed by Sir Charles Barry in the early 1850s and these casts remain the only evidence for its sculptured corbels. Here Richard II's badge of the White Hart gorged and couchant within a palisade supports a shield with the arms of Edward the Confessor.

Cast of a corbel which supported the outer arch of the south window of Westminster Hall   Plaster, made for Sir John Soane, before 1830   Sir John Soane's Museum, M94

The two casts of corbels from the great south window are first recorded in Soane's collection in 1830. Richard II's window was destroyed by Sir Charles Barry in the early 1850s and these casts remain the only evidence for its sculptured corbels. Here Richard II's badge of the White Hart gorged and couchant within a palisade supports a shield with the royal arms, which formerly impaled lost arms on the right.

Cast of a foliage boss from a cornice of Westminster Hall   Plaster, made for Sir John Soane, before 1837
Sir John Soane's Museum, M52

Soane's long association with the Palace of Westminster dated back to 1791 and continued until his death in 1837. The precise position of the originals of the two foliage bosses illustrated here is not recorded. They are similar to the foliage sculptures which still decorate both the interior and exterior cornices of the Hall and belong to Richard II's works of the 1390s.

Cast of a foliage boss from a cornice of Westminster Hall   Plaster, made for Sir John Soane, before 1837
Sir John Soane's Museum, M60

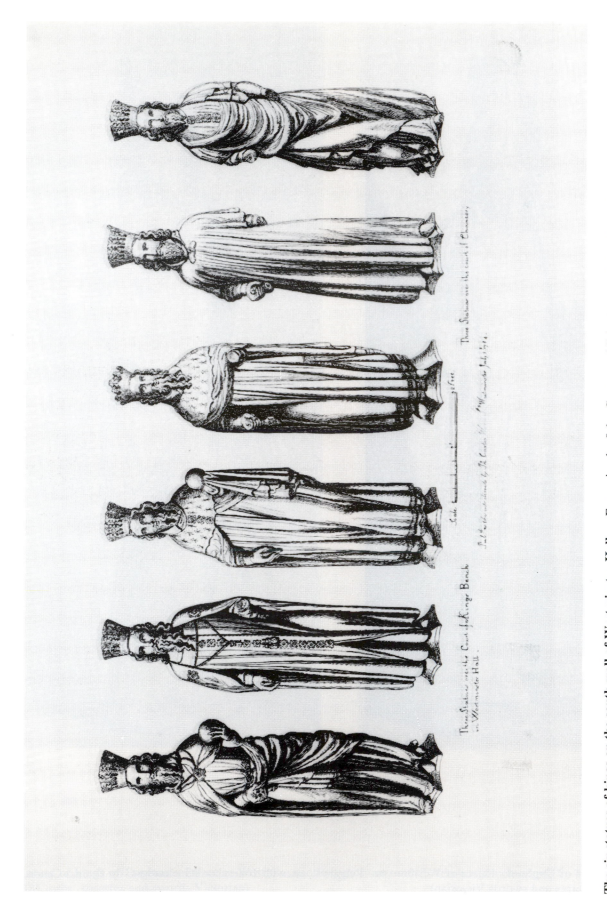

These Statues are the Court of King's Bench in Westminster Hall

These Statues are in the court of Chancery

Scale [illegible] of Feet

Pub'd as the act directs by Ja. Carter N° 4 Westminster July 1784

The six statues of kings on the south wall of Westminster Hall   Engraving by John Carter, published July 1784   Westminster City Archives, Box 58
Carter's original drawings for this engraving are not known to survive. The engraving is precious as it records the order in which the statues were set up in their
niches above the Courts of King's Bench and Chancery in 1784. They had at this time lost most of their attributes, which Sir Charles Barry replaced in the 1850s,
when he also altered the order of the kings.

Conservation of the kings

The statues were heavily limewashed in 1950, following storage during the Second World War. In 1986 English Heritage examined three of the statues and found their surfaces to be in places blistered and friable. By 1989 preliminary consolidation of the surfaces had been undertaken *in situ* and the first three kings were transported to English Heritage's Stone Conservation Studio at Vauxhall.

Analysis identified the Reigate stone of the main figures and the Totternhoe stone of the crowns, which were separately carved and fixed with wooden pegs. The Victorian restorations, principally the sceptres and orbs, were easily recognised. Extensive traces of medieval pigments were found, including red lead, yellow ochre, verdigris and vermilion as well as gilding. Removal of the limewashes was a lengthy process and unexpectedly revealed the fine detail of the carvings. Final consolidation of the surfaces was completed by May 1993. Conservation of the second three kings followed in 1994/5. The six statues are here shown together for the first time since the conservation programme was brought to a successful conclusion. The work was carried out by the English Heritage Stone Conservation Studio and Taylor Pearce Restoration Services Ltd.

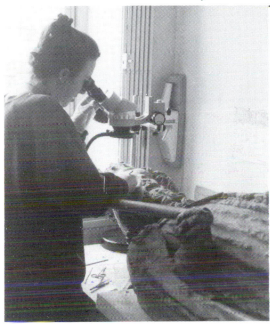

(left) **Removal of the final layer of limewash**
(right) **Halfway through the process of removing the limewash** Photos: Taylor Pearce Restoration Services

Filling-in to support the surface fractures
Photo Taylor Pearce Restoration Services

The north façade of Westminster Hall

Richard II's reconstruction of the main entrance façade of the Hall was underway by Michelmas 1398, apparently under Henry Yevele's supervision. Two flanking towers were added and the old door was replaced by a new one framed by a porch. Rows of niches were installed to either side of the porch and on the bases of the towers. Presumably all the niches, twenty-seven in all, were occupied by statues of kings and queens.

In 1533 most of the statues still survived but by the 17th century the façade had deteriorated, losing many of its sculptures. An ale house and two coffee houses were built against the lower parts of the façade. A preliminary restoration under Wyatt in 1807-8 was severely criticised and followed by a more archaeological campaign under John Soane in 1818-20. However Soane's façade as it still exists today is bare of statues. In 1780 John Carter drew the statues on the façade, and annotated one drawing, 'destroyed next day after this sketch was taken.' Five statues from the façade did survive and currently stand inside Westminster Hall.

North façade of the Hall, as it is today   Photo: Woodmansterne

New Palace Yard from the east, with the north façade of Westminster Hall (*Sala Regalis cum Curia Westmonasterii, vulgo Westminster haall*)   Etching, signed *W. Hollar fecit 1647*   British Museum, P&D 1860-11-9-131

This is one of the eight etchings of London which Hollar made while in Antwerp in 1647. The great gateway of the Palace is shown in the background. The north façade retains its statues both in the lower tier of niches and on the towers, but is already partially obscured by satellite buildings and the wall in front of the Exchequer Court.

North Front of Westminster Hall July 5th 1814   Pen and ink drawing, by John Buckler, 1814   British Library, Add. MS. 36370, fols. 210v–211
By permission of the British Library Board

John Buckler (1770–1851) records the state of the north façade in minute detail. Seven statues were still *in situ* in 1814. The building to the right of the façade is the Court of the Exchequer built in 1569–70 and demolished by Soane in 1823.

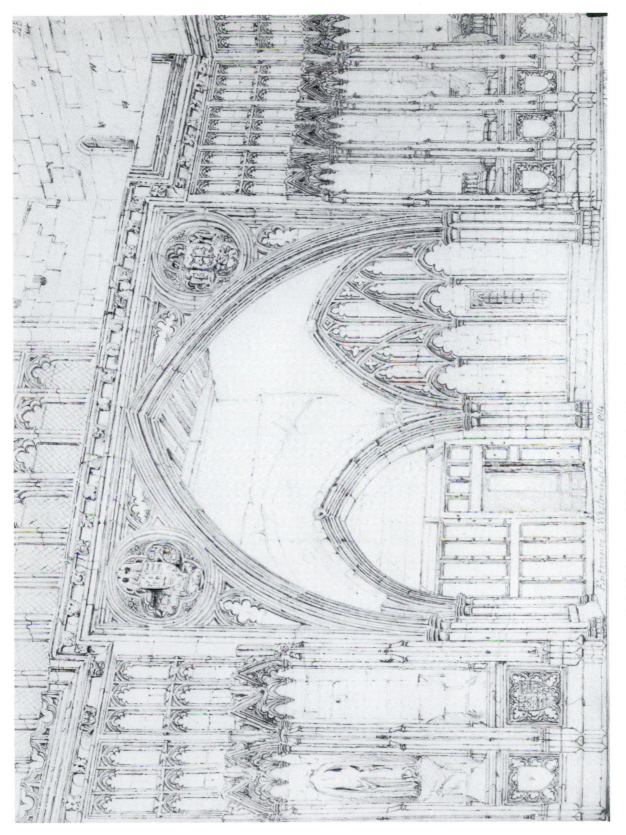

Entrance to Westminster Hall 1814 Pen and ink drawing, by John Buckler, 1814 British Library, Add. MS. 36370, fol. 213
By permission of the British Library Board See illustration on the previous page.

Architect's model of the north façade of Westminster Hall   Wood and painted card, anonymous, 1832-1833
London, private collection.
An inscription inside the porch reads 'This MODEL was begun Novr. 2nd 1832 finished April 22 1833.' The origins and purpose of this model are obscure. It postdates Soane's restoration of 1818-20, but differs in minor details from Soane's façade.

Sketches of the lower storey of the north façade of Westminster Hall   Pencil on paper, John Carter, 1780
Westminster City Archives, Box 58, no. 35
Carter records the elevation, mouldings and ornament of the lower section of the façade to the right of the porch. In 1780 when Carter made these sketches, this part of the façade was enclosed by the walls of a coffee house.

Sketches of the lower storey of the north façade of Westminster Hall   Pencil on paper, John Carter, 1780
Westminster City Archives, Box 58, no. 35
One of Carter's records of details of the façade to the right of the porch - see preceding illustration.

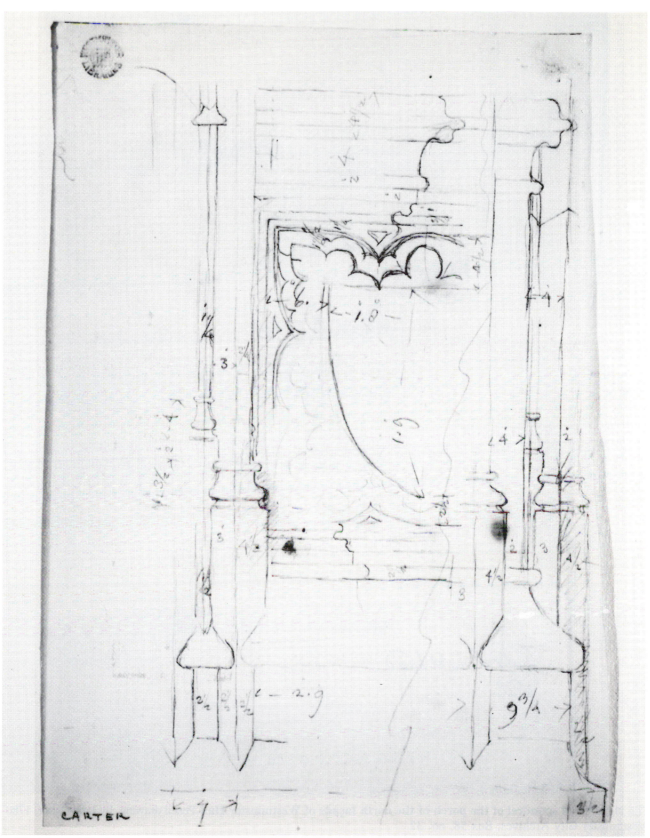

Sketches of the lower storey of the north façade of Westminster Hall   Pencil on paper, John Carter, 1780
Westminster City Archives, Box 58, no. 35
One of Carter's records of the façade to the right of the porch - see the two preceding illustrations.

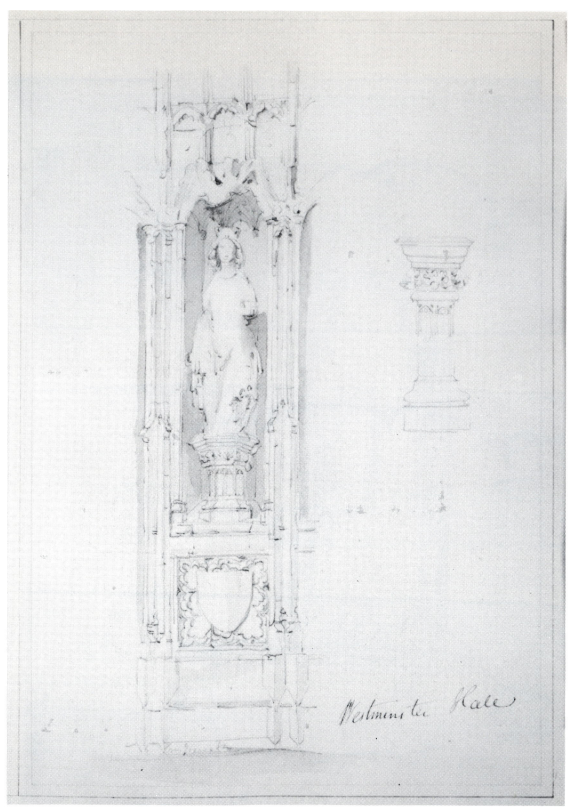

One of the statues on the north façade of Westminster Hall Pen and ink and watercolour, Thomas Pennethorne, about 1814-1816 The Royal Collection © Her Majesty the Queen. Windsor Castle, RL 25824
Several of the watercolours in this album by Thomas Pennethorne are dated 1814-1816. This statue of a queen stood second on the right of the porch, among the seven statues which remained *in situ* until Soane's restoration of 1818-1820. On the right Pennethorne has drawn in detail the socle (plinth) beneath the statue. Some of the socles beneath the façade statues survive in Sir John Soane's Museum.

90

Portrait of Richard II Dean and Chapter of Westminster   Linseed oil medium on panel, the background (originally) stamped chalk decoration with red bole and gilding, anonymous, perhaps mid-1390s with extensive restorations in 1733 and 1866. (Frame designed by Sir Gilbert Scott, made by Clayton and Bell, 1872, for £57 15s.) This famous painting has never been the object of full scientific examination but preliminary work in the National Gallery suggests that in spite of heavy restoration in 1733 by Captain Henry Turner Broome and in 1866 by George Richmond and Henry Merritt, areas of the surface are substantially intact, particularly the head of Richard II. Infra-red spectroscopy revealed bold and extensive underdrawing in a black medium. The throne however appears much altered. The original decorated background of which small areas survive towards the top was largely obliterated in 1866.

No document can with authority be applied to the painting before 1631, when it is mentioned as being in the choir of the Abbey church. However if the head of the king can be relied on, this 'portrait' may be compared to Richard II's effigy in Westminster Abbey, a work begun in 1395. This monumental icon of the monarch has no parallels among the few 'portraits' on panel which have survived north of the Alps from the 14th century.

Heraldry and Badges

Badges

The use of badges as decoration was fashionable in the late 14th century. The white hart was the badge of Richard II and was used for the decoration of the string course along the side of Westminster Hall and the heraldic achievement in the roundel on the north porch of the Hall. Richard II first gave the badge of the white hart to his supporters in 1390. On the interior of the Wilton Diptych (reproduced below), he and the angels surrounding the Virgin wear the badge. On one side of the exterior of the painting the white hart lies on a bed of rosemary; the other side shows the mythical arms of Edward the Confessor impaling the royal arms of England and France.

The white hart also appears on his quadrant and on the Ashanti Ewer (see below). After Richard II had been replaced as King by Henry IV, the swan was used as the Lancastrian royal badge and the collar of SS became the Lancastrian livery collar.

Details from the Wilton Diptych   Photo: National Gallery, NG 4451
(left) The mythical arms of Edward the Confessor impaling the royal arms of England and France
(right) The white hart on a bed of rosemary

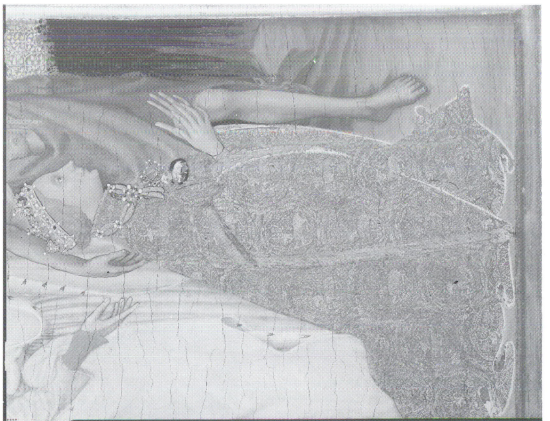

Details from the Wilton Diptych (left) Richard II (right) The Virgin and Child Photo: National Gallery, NG 4451

(left) **Lead badge of a hart**   English, late 14th century   BM MLA 56,6-27,17   H 3.7 cm   W 4 cm
(centre) **Pewter badge of a hart**   English, late 14th century   Lent by J.F.W. Auld   H 3.6 cm   W 3.3 cm
(right) **Lead badge of a swan**   English, early 15th century   BM MLA 1904,7-20,19   H 4.9 cm

The Dunstable Swan Jewel   English, early 15th century   Found in the ruins of the Dominican Friary at Dunstable, Bedfordshire,1965   BM MLA 1966,7-3,1   H 4.3 cm
The jewel, in gold and opaque white enamel, provides an illustration of the nature of the hart badges displayed on the Wilton Diptych. The swan, a badge of the de Bohun family, was adopted by Henry of Lancaster after his marriage to Mary de Bohun. In 1399, Henry of Lancaster replaced Richard II as King of England and the swan was adopted as a Lancastrian royal badge.

The Middleham ring   Gold ring   English, late 14th or early 15th century   Found in the East Park at Middleham in 1990   The Yorkshire Museum YORKM 1992.21   Diameter 2.4 cm
This gold ring is engraved with the word 'sovereynly', meaning in a regal or sovereign-like manner, in the inside. On the outside is the letter S repeated twelve times which would originally have been seen against black enamel. The collar of SS became the Lancastrian livery collar after the accession of Henry IV. The ring may have belonged to Ralph Neville, first Earl of Westmorland, a supporter of Henry IV.

Seals

The Wilton Diptych shows on the back the royal arms of England impaled with those of Edward the Confessor (for Westminster). Richard impaled these arms from 1395 and a number of his supporters also showed the royal arms in this way.

Cast of the seal of Richard II for the Palatinate of Chester   English, between 1395 and 1399   Society of Antiquaries of London casts A12   Diameter 6.3 cm

(left) **Cast of the seal of Edward, Earl of Rutland and Cork, Admiral of England**   English, 1397   Society of Antiquaries of London casts D41   Diameter 5.7 cm

(right) **Cast of the seal of Thomas Arundel, Archbishop of Canterbury**   English, 1397   Society of Antiquaries of London casts C3   H 8.8 cm

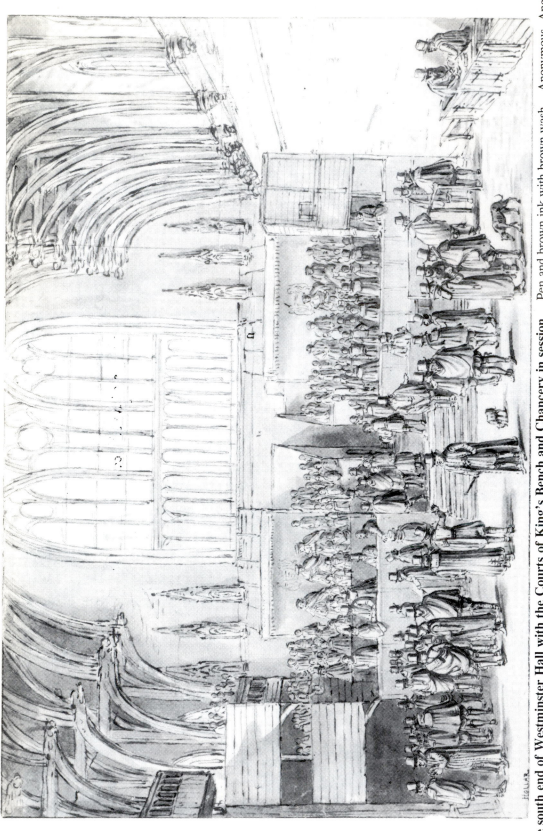

The south end of Westminster Hall with the Courts of King's Bench and Chancery in session   Pen and brown ink with brown wash   Anonymous, Anglo-Dutch School, about 1620   BM P&D 1848-9-11-748

The drawing is one of the earliest interior *views* of Westminster Hall by a competent topographer. The style which is reminiscent of such artists as Willem Buytewech and Jan van de Velde the Younger, as well as the costumes point to the end of the second decade of the 17th century; and although the draughtsmanship is somewhat even and dry, the alterations and *pentimenti* suggest that it is not the work of a copyist. The old attribution to Hollar is not sustainable.

The two Courts already had their allotted places on the dais at the south end of the Hall by the 14th century. Here they are shown in session, with the judges seated under canopies. Spectators are housed in a temporary wooden structure on the left, while the foreground is occupied by groups of lawyers in discussion. The six statues of kings are clearly visible in their niches flanking Richard II's south window.

102

***Internal View of Westminster Hall*, looking south with the Courts of King's Bench and Chancery in the distance**
Preliminary state for an engraving, drawn and engraved by G. Hawkins, published Feb 28th 1801   British Library,
Maps K. Top. XXIV. 24-k   By permission of the British Library Board
George Hawkins Sr. was an architect who exhibited at the Royal Academy between 1795 and 1810. This early state for
his published engraving shows the elaborate hammer-beam structure of Richard II's roof, a late medieval doorway in the
west wall and William Kent's neo-Gothic Law Courts, built in 1739 and heightened in 1755. Of the latter John Carter
in 1800 complained: 'What a farrago of pinnacles and pineapples, pointed compartments and ogee arches, buttresses and
balusters, a Grecian entablature and French ornaments!'

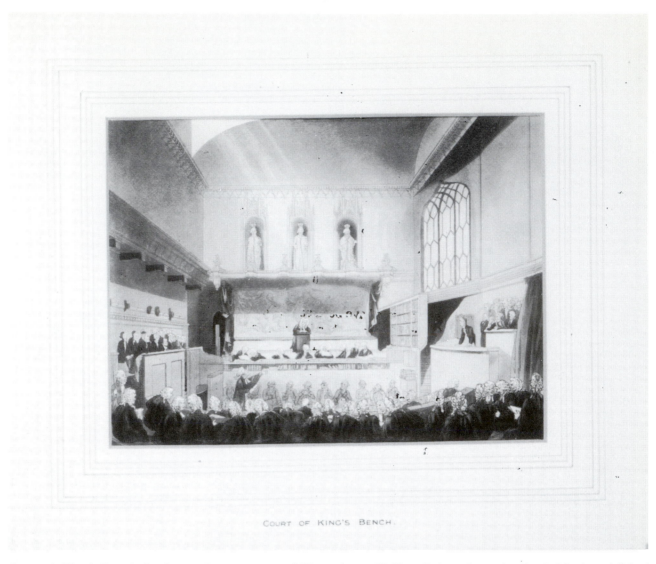

COURT OF KING'S BENCH.

***Court of King's Bench*, in the south-east corner of Westminster Hall**   Coloured aquatint, by J. Bluck, published 1st June 1808
The aquatint after Augustus Pugin and Thomas Rowlandson was published as a plate in Rudolph Ackermann's *Microcosm of London* (1808). Three of the statues of kings are shown in their niches with remains of their polychrome decoration. The Court of King's Bench is in session in the south-east corner of the Hall, within William Kent's Law Courts which were built in 1739 and given a ceiling in 1755. They were demolished in 1821 for George IV's Coronation Banquet.

104

The third and last challenge by the Champion during King George IV's Coronation Banquet in Westminster Hall, 1821 Watercolour, signed *Denis Dighton Military Painter to His Majesty*, about 1821 The Royal Collection © Her Majesty the Queen. Windsor Castle, RL 13630

Denis Dighton (1792-1827) was Military Painter to the Prince Regent and here records the last great ritual Coronation Banquet to take place in the Hall on 19th July, 1821. The traditional Challenge by the Champion is in its final phase. Richard II's south window, side windows and hammer-beam roof look down on one of the most splendid occasions ever to have been held in the Hall.

The interior of Westminster Hall, looking north in the evening   Watercolour by Frederick Nash, between 1837-1856
British Museum, P&D 1856-6-14-69
Frederick Nash (1782-1856) records the Hall after the interior had been restored by Sir Robert Smirke in 1834-1837.
With minor exceptions, the Hall is shown very much as it is today.

The Fire of 1834

On the evening of the 16th October 1834 fire broke out near the House of Lords in the southern area of the Palace, where workmen were burning the Old Tally Office Sticks. The fire spread quickly throughout the night and, with the exception of the Great Hall, left the palace a smouldering wreck the next morning. The general public flocked to watch the spectacle, from the streets and bridges, and from boats on the river.

Many artists recorded the event, and broadsheets printed vivid descriptions. The medievalists approved the destruction of the more recent buildings; Pugin wrote that it was, 'a glorious sight to see Wyatt's composition mullions and cement pinnacles and battlements flying and cracking... the old walls stood triumphantly amidst the scene of ruin.' Artists were commissioned to record the ruins and some of their views are illustrated here.

In the years that followed, the debate conducted between those who wished to preserve the old structures and those favouring demolition and the creation of a new overall plan was won by the latter. In 1849 the foundation stone of Barry's new Palace was laid and most of the vestiges of the earlier palace vanished.

Detail from *The Fire in Old Palace Yard*   Colour lithograph, by William Heath (published 1834)

Westminster from the river during the night of 16th October 1834   Watercolour and bodycolour on card, signed *P.T. Cameron*, about 1834
Guildhall Library, Corporation of London
The east front of St. Stephen's Chapel is in the centre, the Painted Chamber to its left.

Westminster from the river during the night of 16th October 1834   Hand-coloured lithograph, anonymous, 'Published by G.S. Tregear, 96 Cheapside, London,' 1834 Westminster City Archives, Box 57, no. 15

News of the fire spread almost as fast as the fire itself. This popular print shows spectators enjoying the drama from Westminster Bridge and from boats on the river. The floating fire pump, the Sun Fire, can be seen near the palace. It arrived too late to do more than contain the fire within the gutted buildings.

DREADFUL FIRE, AND TOTAL DESTRUCTION OF BOTH HOUSES OF PARLIAMENT.

We this day record with unfeigned regret the destruction by fire of the two Houses of Parliament, and most of the large and magnificent ranges of offices and buildings connected with them. This lamentable conflagration commenced between the hours of 6 and 7 last night, and originated in some neglect or accident of the workmen employed in making alterations in the Library of the Lords, and who had just left their work in that part of the building. The Houses of Lords and Commons are utterly destroyed, with the library rooms of the former, and we believe of the latter. A considerable portion of the offices and rooms, together with the Painted Chamber (of Conference) of the Lords, is wholly gutted by the fire. The houses of Mr Ley, and the intermediate habitations of the principal offices of Parliament, situated between the Lords' Journal-office and the Speaker's house, were completely burned between the hours of 9 and 11. A deal of the furniture and books were saved, and stored in the gardens. At a late hour the Speaker's house was partially gutted, those rooms with the large gothic windows looking on the water, and the wing immediately adjoining, were completely destroyed. The conflagration ultimately extended all round the new front buildings of the Lords, utterly consuming the rooms of the Lord Chancellor, Mr Courtnay, and other offices ranging round Hayes's coffee-house. The latter premises also are wholly destroyed. We fear that the records of the House of Commons have most severely suffered, if not been entirely destroyed.

Further Particulars.

The fire was first discovered in the lobby of the House of Lords. From thence it communicated to the left wing of the building burning with irresistible fury. A few minutes after 7 the roof fell in with a tremendous crash. The fire, the fierceness of which was heightened by the increasing freshness of the breeze, then communicated to the House of Commons, and the whole range of buildings was soon wrapped in one blaze. The scene at this time was grand & terrific. The flames shot up to a great height and obscured the light of the moon. Not only the streets in the vicinity, but the different bridges, were covered with immense multitudes, gazing with mingled awe and admiration on the scene of destruction.

Soon after the breaking out of the fire, Sir John Hobhouse arrived, and gave directions for the immediate removal of the public records, an operation which he actively and anxiously superintended. They were put into all sorts of vehicles, hackney-coaches, cabs, waggons, &c.

While the turret in the western corner was in flames, Lord Frederick Fitzclarence, with several policemen and soldiers, were in the uppermost room. They were not at first aware of their danger; but as their perilous state was discovered by persons without a fireman's ladder, which is formed of parts that slide on each other, was instantly put up to the top window, and they descended, Lord Frederick being the last who got upon the ladder. At this time a great quantity of water was thrown into this quarter of the building, but it had little effect, and the flames gradually descended to the first story.

A more wide-spreading or imposing fire was never witnessed in the Metropolis. The associations connected with the ancient Chapel of St. Stephens and the House of Lords, every apartment of which recalls some great historical event— the vivid view of the rapid flames as they rolled round this large frontage of public buildings driven by the shifting wind —the glare of the towering flames, the volumes of smoke which mixed with the raging element—the repeated crashes of the falling roofs, all combined to impress the crowds who attended the fire with feelings never to be forgotten. In the midst of this striking scene, the Chapel of HENRY the SEVENTH and Westminster Abbey appeared enveloped in flames; and the reflection of the fire on the turrets, and delicate tracery of the architecture of the Chapel, produced a singular effect. The view of the Thames was not less remarkable. The river and bridges were covered with people, large parties contemplating the awful scene, and the water, like a mirror, reflecting the glare of the conflagration.

Dispatches, communicating this distressing intelligence were sent to different parts of the country, and his Majesty was informed of it within two hours of the fire breaking out.

We rejoice to state that Westminster Hall is saved.

J. Catnach, Printer, 2, & 3, Monmouth-court, 7 Dials.

Dreadful Fire, And Total Destruction Of Both Houses Of Parliament   Broadsheet, with woodcut, published by 'J. Catnach, Printer, 2, & 3, Monmouth-court, 7 Dials,' 17th October 1834   Guildhall Library, Corporation of London
This is one of the broadsheets which were sold after the fire, describing the more sensational details. The presence of the Life Guards, Grenadier and Coldstream Guards to control the crowds, and the saving of records are the focus of this popular print.

Burning of the Houses of Parliament Watercolour, by J.M.W. Turner, 1834 Tate Gallery, D27847 (Turner Bequest CCLXXXIII-2- bequeathed by the artist, 1856)

Of all the artists who recorded the great fire of 1834, Turner was the one who succeeded in leaving an indelible impression. In a series of celebrated paintings and watercolours he captured the chaos and fear which the fire aroused, as well as the inferno of the flames and smoke.

Westminster from the river after the fire Oil on canvas, anonymous, about 1834 Palace of Westminster, 2806
Formerly attributed to David Roberts (1796-1864), there is a second version of this painting in the Museum of London. The smouldering ruins of the palace are recorded on the morning after the night of the 16th October 1834. The east gable of St. Stephen's Chapel is prominent in the centre. Two artists are sketching the ruins from a boat in the left foreground.

The fire in Westminster Hall   Pen and ink and watercolour, by G.B. Campion, 1834   Palace of Westminster, 1669 (Presented by the Fire Protection Association, 1972)

The Hall was the only major part of the Palace which survived the night of the 16th October. Here the fire fighters can be seen climbing ladders and dousing the great roof timbers, while hand water pumps are being operated in the foreground. The six statues of kings are dimly to be made out on either side of the south window.

113

View of the Painted Chamber looking into the House of Lords   Pen and ink and watercolour, signed *R.W. Billings*,
Oct 25th 1834   Palace of Westminster, 1666 (presented by Sir Leicester Harmsworth, M.P.)
R.W. Billings (1813-1874) executed many of the drawings of the Palace after the fire, which were engraved for Brayley
and Britton's *Westminster* (1836). This is one of them. The Painted Chamber has lost its roof and Billings shows the west
and north walls, with the House of Lords (Court of Requests) beyond. An artist is sketching the ruins at a desk on the
right, while masons are shown at work in the Chamber and on a ladder on the walls.

The ruined crypt of St. Stephen's Chapel, after the fire Pen and ink and watercolour, by George Moore, about 1834   Palace of Westminster, Walker no. 10 (presented by Sir John Wolfe-Barry, K.C.B.)

The crypt of the Chapel is shown looking south-west, with the lierne vaults of its two western bays intact. The vault bosses still have traces of paint. Fragments of architectural mouldings are lying on the floor. The crypt is the only part of the chapel which survives today, although it was extensively rebuilt by Edward Middleton Barry in the 1860s.

The remains of St. Stephen's Chapel after the fire, from the south-east   Pen and ink and watercolour, by A. Maqueline, about 1834   Museum of London, A12137

On the left is the north-east angle of the Painted Chamber. The walls of St. Stephen's Chapel are substantially intact. Proposals for a new House of Commons with a restored St. Stephen's were rejected, and only the crypt survived in the new Houses of Parliament.